NEWTisms ★★★

THE WIT AND WISDOM
OF
Newt Gingrich

COMPILED BY
GEOFF RODKEY

POCKET BOOKS
New York   London   Toronto   Sydney   Tokyo   Singapore

An *Original* Publication of POCKET BOOKS

POCKET BOOKS, a division of Simon & Schuster Inc.
1230 Avenue of the Americas, New York, NY 10020

Copyright © 1995 by Geoff Rodkey

ISBN: 0-671-53533-1

First Pocket Books trade paperback printing February 1995

10 9 8 7 6 5 4 3 2 1

POCKET and colophon are registered trademarks of Simon & Schuster Inc.

Cover photo by Andrew Innerarity/AP

Printed in the U.S.A.

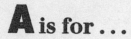# A is for …

AFFIRMATIVE ACTION

"People who want some kind of quota ... based on your racial background should be forced to debate in public their vision of America. ... I would make clear that I oppose quotas explicitly because I favor an integrated America."

The New York Times, 12/10/92

A is for ...

AMBITION

"I have an enormous personal ambition. I want to shift the entire planet. And I'm doing it."

—spoken in 1985. Quoted in
The Washington Post, 12/20/94

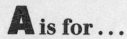# A is for ...

THE AMERICAN CIVIL LIBERTIES UNION

"The ACLU ... verges on paranoia, is almost psychopathic in its commitment to a vision of an American danger that simply does not exist, that is literally impossible except in the most esoteric salons of the liberal elite of this country."

The Congressional Record, 2/7/84

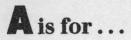

A is for . . .

THE AMERICAN PEOPLE

"The American people are pretty smart. If they can't affect something, they tend to ignore it."

National Review, 5/28/90

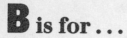 **B** is for . . .

BIG BIRD AND BARNEY

"Big Bird makes money; Barney makes money. These are profit-making centers. They would survive fine. I understand why the elite wants the money [for public TV], but I think they ought to be honest. These are a bunch of rich, upper-class people who want their toy to play with."

—Broadcast on a taped interview on C-Span aired 1/2/95 (*New York Post*, 1/3/95)

B is for . . .

BIMBOS, REAL AND IMAGINED

"That was no bimbo. That was my wife."

> —attributed to Gingrich upon hearing that a Utah paper had published a report of him kissing a "bimbo" on the street in Washington. *National Review,* 6/30/89

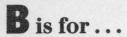

. . . BITCH

" 'She's a bitch.' About the only thing he ever said about her."

> —attributed to Gingrich by his mother, Kathleen Gingrich, about First Lady Hillary Clinton in response to a question posed by Connie Chung during an interview in which Chung prodded Mrs. Gingrich by saying, "Why don't you just whisper it to me, just between you and me." Broadcast on CBS's "Eye to Eye with Connie Chung," 1/5/95

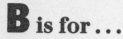# B is for . . .

BLOOD RELATIVES, AND THEIR EFFECT ON ONE'S POLITICAL BELIEFS

"My uncle . . . taught me to smile at Eisenhower on the television and to turn Adlai Stevenson off."

> —speaking in 1974 about the political aspect of his upbringing.
> *The Washington Post*, 12/18/94

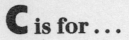

C is for . . .

CAMPAIGN FINANCE REFORM AND THE COST OF BEER ADS

"[Democrats] have rigged the game better than Noriega. . . . The fact is, in almost any other business in America we spend vastly more money trying to communicate with the American people than we do in campaigns. Look at the cost of advertising beer."

Mother Jones, 10/89

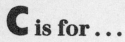

C is for ...

CHANGE

"The only way you get change is to
vote Republican."

The New York Times, 11/8/94

C is for . . .

CLINTON

"[Clinton would] be a good guy to have a beer with. He'd be a great frat president."

The New Republic, 11/28/94

"What you got was Dukakis with a southern accent."

—on Clinton's election.
The New York Times, 7/24/94

C is for ...

CLINTON

"[Bill Clinton] has to decide. Does he want to cooperate with a rising populist majority, or does he want to go down in history as the last defender of the old order?"

Time, 11/7/94

"Counterculture McGoverniks ... left-wing elitists."

—describing the Clintons and the White House staff, respectively.
The Washington Post, 11/10/94

C is for...

COOPERATION

"I am very prepared to cooperate with the Clinton Administration. I am not prepared to compromise."

The New York Times, 11/12/94

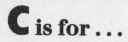

C is for . . .

THE COUNTERCULTURE

"We have to say to the counterculture:
'Nice try. You failed. You're wrong.' "

The New York Times, 11/12/94

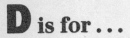

D is for ...

A DEBATE WITH A BIGGER BUDGET THAN FRANK GIFFORD

"Imagine a national debate on social security, defense, foreign policy, health care, or educational policy, with the same budget as ABC spends on Monday Night Football."

—from an article coauthored by Gingrich's wife Marianne. *The Futurist,* 12/81

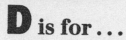

D is for . . .

THE DECAY OF AMERICAN LIFE

"We ought to ask ourselves if we are really willing to settle for the decay of the American way of life."

The Futurist, 8/81

D is for . . .

DECAPITATING BUREAUCRATS

"Nobody on the battle line would notice that they were gone if you decapitated the top twelve thousand bureaucrats and started over with a new model."

Mother Jones, 10/89

D is for . . .

THE DEMOCRATIC LEADERSHIP

"The Democratic Leaders are sick. . . .
They are so consumed by their own
power, by a Mussolini-like ego, that
their willingness to run over normal
human beings and to destroy honest
institutions is unending."

Mother Jones, 10/89

D is for ...

DEMOCRATIC DISNEYLAND

"Now comes the Democratic platform [of 1980], appearing to emanate from a fantasyland as it, one, takes credit for things it says are fine but which are not and, two, places blame for what it cannot explain on previous administrations and foreign powers."

The Congressional Record, 5/21/80

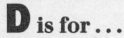

D is for ...

THE DIFFERENCE BETWEEN LIBERALS AND CONSERVATIVES

"We're prepared to place our trust in the people to reshape the government. Our liberal friends place their trust in the government to reshape the people."

The New York Times, 10/27/94

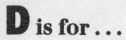

D is for ...

THE DIVORCE-PAPERS-IN-THE-HOSPITAL STORY

"My recollection is a little different. What passes between two people ... It's just very difficult, very painful."

> —responding to the allegation that he came to his wife's hospital room carrying divorce papers while she was recovering from cancer surgery. *Esquire*, 10/89

D is for . . .

BOB DOLE

"The tax collector of the welfare state."

> —Gingrich's oft-quoted mid-'80s appraisal of Dole. *Mother Jones,* 10/89

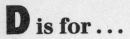

D is for ...

DUMB

"Very, very dumb."

> —on the possibility that Clinton might try
> to stand in the way of the conservative
> agenda. *The Washington Post,* 11/10/94

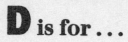

D is for ...

THE DEMOCRATS' DUMB IDEAS

"Our role in the [Republican] minority is to offer new ideas, to offer intelligent criticism of their dumb ideas."

The Atlantic, 6/93

E is for ...

EDUCATION

"We must shift the focus of education from teaching to learning. . . . One experiment worth trying would be to offer a $500 bonus for any child who enters the first grade reading at a fourth-grade level."

The Futurist, 6/85

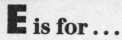

E is for . . .

ENEMIES

"The enemy of normal Americans."

> —on how Clinton Democrats should be
> portrayed. *The Washington Post,*
> 10/14/94

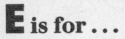

E is for ...

ETHNIC CONFLICT

"We are creating a time bomb of misery in this country ... it is in many ways essentially an ethnic time bomb, because, despite the efforts of the last generation, it is still generally true: The blacks are the last hired and first fired ... a free society cannot long endure if a large portion of its people feel rejected and outcast and left alone."

The Congressional Record, 4/23/80

E is for ...

EVIL

"People like me are what stand between us and Auschwitz. I see evil around me every day."

The Washington Post, 12/18/94
(*Atlanta Constitution*, January 1994)

F is for . . .

FAME

"I am now a famous person . . . I represent real power."

—spoken in 1985, quoted in
The Washington Post, 12/20/94

F is for . . .

FASCINATING THE OPPOSITION

"I clearly fascinate them."

—on Democrats' reaction to him.
The Washington Post, 10/20/94

F is for . . .

FOREIGN POLICY

"Our primary goal in foreign policy is very simple: It is our intention to survive no matter what the level of chaos on the rest of this planet."

The Congressional Record, 9/24/80

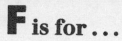

F is for ...

FUN

"I'm having fun. I'm doing everything
I want to do."

The Atlantic, 6/93

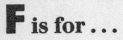

F is for . . .

FUTURE GENERATIONS

"I'll keep trying to recruit another
generation and train another
generation so that when I'm too tired
to keep doing this, they'll be ready to
step in."

The Washington Post, 12/18/94
(*Atlanta Constitution*, January 1994)

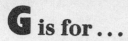

G is for ...

GETTING UP AGAIN

"You knock me on the mat and I get up again."

Esquire, 10/89

G is for . . .

GOVERNMENT

"There are two realities to the current system: one is the government is trying to cheat you. And the second is the government is lying to you about what it's doing."

Mother Jones, 10/89

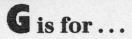

G is for ...

GOVERNMENT

"Government of, by, and for the people has become Government of, by, and for Government."

The Congressional Record, 5/21/80

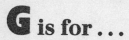

G is for ...

LYNDON JOHNSON'S GREAT SOCIETY PROGRAMS, WHICH DIDN'T WORK

"... the Great Society [programs] ... and the counterculture values ... are a disaster. They have ruined the poor. They create a culture of poverty and a culture of violence. And they have to be replaced thoroughly."

The New York Times, 11/12/94

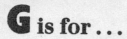

G is for ...

"GUNSMOKE"

" 'Gunsmoke' normally had very little violence, it was really sort of a soap opera with cowboys and people sat around the saloon and talked with Kitty, and 'Doc' dropped by. . . . The show did not begin with 12 people gang-raping Kitty or the marshal saying, 'Gee, we cannot get involved, the ACLU will get upset.' "

The Congressional Record, 2/2/84

H is for . . .

HEALTH CARE REFORM

"They [the Clinton Administration] really are left-wing elitists and they really thought the country didn't get it and therefore it was their job to give the country the Government that they thought the country needed, even if they didn't want it. That's the whole history of the health plan."

The New York Times, 11/10/94

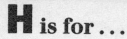# H is for ...

A HEALTHY DEBATE

"Both my family and my party are strong enough to have healthy, spirited debates."

> —when asked about his daughter's endorsement of abortion rights. *The New York Times Magazine,* 8/23/92

H is for ...

HOW HARD LIFE IS

"I think life is normally hard, and it's the good moments that are the aberration. A healthy society starts out saying: Life is hard."

The Washington Post, 12/19/94

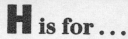is for ...

BEING A HOSTAGE TO THE DECISIONS OF OTHERS

"If you live your life as a hostage to everybody else's decision, you either have to live a very narrow life or you have to spend a lot of time in pain."

—on his parents' refusal to give their blessing to his first marriage.
The Washington Post, 12/18/94

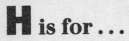 is for ...

THE HOUSE OF REPRESENTATIVES

"The House is a corrupt institution."

Esquire, 10/89

"I'm a creature of the House."

The Atlantic, 6/93

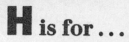

H is for ...

HYPERBOLE

"The thing that shocks people ... is that I mean what I say. I don't use hyperbole."

Mother Jones, 10/89

I is for …

IGNORANCE IN THE OVAL OFFICE

"If the Soviet empire still existed, I'd be terrified. The fact is, we can afford a fairly ignorant presidency now."

The Atlantic, 6/93

I is for ...

INTENSITY

"I'm much more intense, much more persistent, much more willing to take risks to get it done. Since they think it is their job to run the plantation, it shocks them that I'm actually willing to lead the slave rebellion."

The Washington Post, 10/20/94

I is for ...

IRREPRESSIBLE

"[I feel like] an irrepressible 4-year-old."

The Washington Post, 12/21/94

J is for...

JANE FONDA

"We have been too timid. We have not been willing to stand toe-to-toe with the Ralph Naders and the Jane Fondas, with the people . . . who assume with a sneer that if you do it in uniform it is bad but if you do it in welfare it is good."

The Congressional Record, 9/24/80

J is for ...

JODIE FOSTER

"I heard a radio news report that Jodie Foster had been found with cocaine coming [into] the United States, but there was 'insufficient quantity to arrest her. . . .' Now . . . what if I described to you a nation in which a cocaine user would be let go, but seven parents who wanted to send their children to a school so they could learn about God would be arrested. That would sound like the Soviet Union, like Nazi Germany or a degenerate dictatorship."

The Congressional Record, 2/7/84

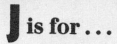

J is for . . .

JOHN WAYNE

"I . . . saw 'The Sands of Iwo Jima'
four times in one day."

—describing life at age ten.
The Washington Post, 12/18/94

K is for ...

KILLING GEORGE BUSH'S TAX PLAN

"[Bush] said with as much pain as I've heard from a politician, 'You are killing us, you are just killing us.' Even today it brings tremendous emotion to me. I mean I just want to cry."

> —describing a confrontation with Bush over Gingrich's refusal to support Bush's 1990 budget. *The Washington Post,* 12/21/94

L is for ...

LEADERSHIP

"Leadership means taking risks.
You're fighting a war. It is a war for
power."

> —to a group of young Republicans.
> *Esquire*, 10/89

L is for ...

THE LEFT

"The values of the Left cripple human beings, weaken cities, make it difficult for us to in fact survive as a country. ... The Left in America is to blame for most of the current, major diseases which have struck this society."

Mother Jones, 10/89

L is for . . .

LOVE AT FIRST SIGHT

"I'm going to marry her."

—attributed to Gingrich by a former
classmate, reportedly spoken on the
first day of a high school geometry
class taught by his future first wife.
The Washington Post, 12/18/94

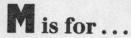
M is for ...

MARITAL PROBLEMS

"It was a tragedy. I wish it had not happened. I mean you go through life and sometimes things happen. . . . In a different world maybe it would have worked differently."

> —talking about his first marriage.
> *The Washington Post,* 12/19/94

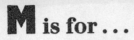 **M** is for . . .

THE MEDIA

"It is much easier to communicate, in the current generation of news media, about scandal than about substance."

The New York Times Magazine, 8/23/92

M is for . . .

MEDIA ELITE

"I don't have a prayer of getting my message out with the elite media. So my assumption is that people who share our values want to help get our message out."

—on his use of Rush Limbaugh and the Christian Coalition's broadcasts to deliver his message. *The New York Times,* 11/10/94

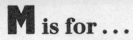**M** is for . . .

MODERATE

"I am a moderate."

> —spoken to reporters on his election
> night in 1978. Quoted in
> *The Washington Post,* 12/19/94

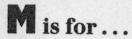

M is for . . .

MUDSLINGING

"I personally do not intend to stay in a politics dominated by smearing and mudslinging—a politics which has all too often been characteristic of recent years in this country."

The Congressional Record, 10/20/83

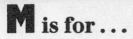 **M** is for . . .

MULTICULTURAL

"[The Democrats promote] a multicultural, nihilistic hedonism that is inherently destructive of a healthy society."

> —spoken at the 1992 Republican National Convention. *The New York Times*, 8/19/92

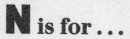is for . . .

THE NEW HAMPSHIRE STATE MOTTO

"New Hampshire's slogan is 'Live Free Or Die'; it is not 'Live Free or Whine.' "

The New York Times, 11/12/94

. . . NASTY

"One of the great problems in the Republican Party is that we don't encourage you to be nasty."

—Speech to college Republicans, June 24, 1978 (quoted in *Newsweek* 11/21/94)

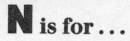 **N** is for . . .

THE NIGHTLY NEWS

"The evening news is the natural
result of the welfare state."

The New Republic, 11/7/94

. . . NEW SPEAKER OF THE HOUSE

"I know I'm a very partisan figure, but
I really hope today that I can speak for
a minute to my friends in the
Democratic Party as well as my own
colleagues, speak to the country, . . . I
hope we can have a real dialogue."

—Speech on the opening day of the 104th
Congress, 1/4/95 (as transcribed by
The New York Times)

O is for . . .

OPPONENTS

"A weird left-wing actor."

> —describing Ben Jones, Gingrich's opponent in the 1994 election and the man who formerly played Cooter on "The Dukes of Hazzard." *The New York Times,* 11/7/94

. . . ORPHANAGES

"I would ask her to go to Blockbuster and rent the Mickey Rooney movie 'Boys Town.'"

> —Gingrich's response to a question on NBC's "Meet the Press" when asked about Hillary Clinton's criticism of his controversial statement that children of teen-age mothers on welfare should be put in orphanages, *Reuters,* 12/4/94

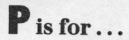

P is for . . .

A PARTISAN PAST

"I've been seen as a partisan, and I am a partisan. [But] that era is over."

The New York Times, 10/27/94

P is for . . .

POVERTY

"No one must fall beneath a certain level of poverty, even if we must give away food and money."

The Futurist, 6/85

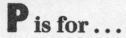

P is for ...

PRAYER IN THE SCHOOLS

"I asked the ... Democratic whip why
we could not bring up prayer in
school next week. ... He said, 'Well,
we brought it up once before, in
1969. ...' I suggested that we could
bring it up more often than once in a
generation."

The Congressional Record, 2/2/84

P is for . . .

PRAYER IN THE SCHOOLS

"In other words, you could be invited to the Marxist study club, you could wear a Marxist T-shirt; that is freedom of speech. You could be invited to a Gay Rights activist meeting, you could wear a Gay Rights T-shirt; that is freedom of speech. But if you wanted to wear a T-shirt that celebrated God or if you wanted to join a club which celebrated religion, that was not permissible; that was not freedom of speech."

—discussing the separation of church and state in public schools.
The Congressional Record, 3/1/84

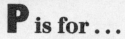

P is for ...

PROMISING TO BE PLEASANT

"I will be somewhat less confrontational, and somewhat less abrasive in the future."

—spoken in 1985. Quoted in
The Washington Post, 12/21/94

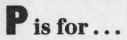

P is for . . .

PUNISHMENT

"A society which punishes violence and a society that is emphatic about right and wrong tends to have less sickness and less violence."

The New York Times, 11/10/94

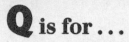

Q is for . . .

QUALITY OF LIFE

"We are at the edge of losing this civilization. You get two more generations of what we had for the last 20 years and we're in desperate trouble."

The Washington Post, 12/18/94
(Atlanta Constitution, 1/94)

R is for ...

RONALD REAGAN AND RACE RELATIONS

"Reagan was literally unknowing in the whole zone of race relations. It wasn't part of his world, and he was very, very insensitive to it. For eight years we communicated a symbol of insensitivity."

Mother Jones, 10/89

R is for ...

REALITY

"[The Clinton White House] can either decide to accommodate reality or they can decide to repudiate reality. That's their choice."

The New York Times, 11/10/94

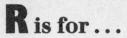

R is for ...

RENEWAL AND REDIRECTION

"Renew American civilization [and] redirect the fate of the human race."

—describing his goals.
The New York Times, 10/27/94

R is for ...

REPUBLICAN IDEAS

"I think it is an interesting historical turning point that for the first time in my lifetime it is the Republican Party which has the idea, the initiative, the issues, the research and it is the former majority party which is in decay."

The Congressional Record, 2/11/80

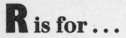

R is for . . .

REVOLUTIONARY

"I am essentially a revolutionary."

The New York Times Magazine, 8/23/92

S is for . . .

SAVANAROLA

"I don't think I'm a Savanarola. I don't think I have any great interest in running around and finding sin."

The New York Times Magazine, 8/23/92

S is for . . .

SCAPEGOATS

"The public has to have a bad person.
It's the nature of Western culture."

Mother Jones, 10/89

S is for ...

SIN

"In the 1970s, things happened—period. That's the most I'll ever say."

> —on allegations that he was unfaithful to his first wife. *The Washington Post,* 12/19/94

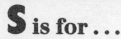

"I start with the assumption that all human beings sin and that all human beings are in fact human. . . . So all I'll say is that I've led a human life."

> —discussing allegations that he committed adultery. *The Washington Post,* 12/19/94

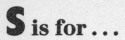

S is for ...

SPECIAL INTERESTS AND SOCIALISM

"The idea that a congressman would be tainted by accepting money from private industry or private sources is essentially a socialist argument."

Mother Jones, 10/89

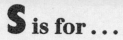

S is for . . .

STEPFATHER

"It was a classic pychodrama."

—on his relationship with his stepfather.
The Washington Post, 12/18/94

T is for ...

TAKE A MESSAGE

"[Tell the President I'll call him back.]"

—attributed. *Time*, 11/21/94

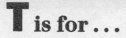

T is for ...

THE THIRD WORLD

"We must have adequate professional forces to impose our will on the Third World. Let me repeat that, because it is a very unfashionable thing to say. ... There are those moments in life when we are going to disagree with other people, and it is my belief that when we fundamentally disagree with somebody we should win."

The Congressional Record, 9/24/80

T is for . . .

TRAIN WRECKS

"My message [to the Democrats] is . . . 'You want to avoid this kind of train wreck, you're going to call us in at the beginning . . . have conferences that are honest . . . and . . . do this thing with dignity. And, if you don't, every chance I get to wreck the train I'm going to wreck it. And when you get tired of looking stupid in public we'll talk.' "

> —on the battles over the '94 crime bill.
> *The New Yorker*, 9/5/94

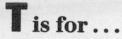

T is for ...

TODAY'S TROUBLED TEENS

"It is impossible to maintain civilization with 12-year-olds having babies, 15-year-olds killing each other, 17-year-olds dying of AIDS and with 18-year-olds ending up with diplomas they can barely read."

The New York Times, 11/12/94

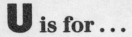

U is for . . .

UNPROVEN RUMORS

"She's not young enough or pretty enough to be the wife of the president. And besides, she has cancer."

> —attributed to Gingrich by former friend
> L.H. Carter and vehemently denied by
> Gingrich himself on why Gingrich
> wanted to divorce his first wife.
> *The Washington Post*, 12/19/94

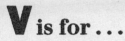

V is for . . .

THE VACATIONS OF THE FUTURE

"As people grow wealthier and the cost of space transportation comes down, spending a week's vacation on a space station or a honeymoon on the moon may become commonplace."

The Futurist, 6/85

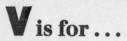 is for ...

VIOLENCE BY WHITE HOUSE AIDES

"... I thought that [George] Stephanopoulous would have just as soon shot all of us."

—on the '94 crime bill negotiations.
The New Yorker, 9/5/94

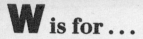 **W** is for . . .

WALKING OUT OF THE ROOM

"I believe there are a lot of things you
can make work if you're always
willing to walk out of the room."

The Washington Post, 12/21/94

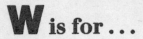

W is for . . .

WASHINGTON

"[Washington] is a city which is like a sponge. It absorbs waves of change, and it slows them down, and it softens them, and then one morning they cease to exist."

The New York Times, 11/15/94

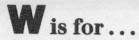# W is for ...

WEIRD THINGS COMING OUT OF WASHINGTON

"You're gonna see weird things coming out of this city over the next few years, because you're watching the death throes of the machine, and you're watching its power to smear, and its power to intimidate."

Mother Jones, 10/89

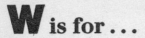 **W** is for . . .

THE WELFARE STATE

"The fatal problem of the welfare
state . . . [is] the welfare state creates
the loser. You didn't have losers in
immigrant America of the 1800s."

The Washington Post, 12/19/94

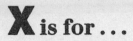

X is for ...

EX-SURGEON GENERAL JOCELYN ELDERS

"They [Americans] don't really want to have a Surgeon General who's an overt anti-Catholic bigot."

The New York Times, 11/10/94

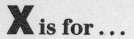

X is for ...

THE NE**X**T GENERATION

"We will not make it through your lifetime without radical change. You're either going to force the changes, or your generation is going to suffer a long, steady decline in the quality of life."

The New York Times Magazine, 8/23/92

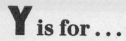

Y is for . . .

YEARS FROM NOW

"Our grandchildren . . . will make calls to any spot on the globe—and perhaps to friends on space habitats or on the moon—as routinely as we now call friends across town."

The Futurist, 6/85

Z is for ...

ZEITGEIST

"I think we are, in fact, at the beginning of a new age. I think the sign for the future is not one of despair, of decay, of collapse, but rather one of real hope, real optimism, of real change. I would suggest as we end this quarter century of domination by the Democratic Party that we are at the beginning of a real cultural, intellectual, and political struggle over the future of this country."

The Congressional Record, 12/20/79